How They Started

Other books in the How They Started series

How They Started
How 30 good ideas became great businesses

How They Started: Global Brands
How 21 good ideas became great global businesses

How They Started in Tough Times
How 25 companies started and thrived during an economic crisis

How
They
Started
Pocket Edition

crimson

How They Started: Pocket Edition
First published in Great Britain in 2011 by
Crimson Publishing, a division of Crimson Business Ltd
Westminster House, Kew Road, Richmond, Surrey TW9 2ND

© Crimson Publishing 2011

Some of the content of this book was previously published as *How They Started* in 2009

A catalogue record for this book is available from the British Library.

ISBN 978 1 85458 689 6

Typeset by IDSUK (Data Connection) Ltd
Printed and bound in Italy by LEGO Print SpA, Trento

Contents

Foreword

When we started Innocent we discovered just what an emotional rollercoaster starting a business is. The three of us quit good jobs to pursue an idea that we believed could go somewhere. Eventually it did, but it took a lot of time, determination and patience. It's not an easy journey.

Like a lot of people just starting out, we hadn't read much about how other people had set up their own businesses. We would have found this book a huge help – if only to strengthen our resolve that we weren't completely mad to carry on!

Above all what I love about this book is the passion and commitment from so many people who've taken an idea and overcome all kinds of obstacles to build a thriving business. Each story is different, some very personal, some surprising, but all are encouraging.

If you go on to start your own business after reading this, I wish you the best of luck with it. And remember, enjoy it, and keep the main thing the main thing.

Richard Reed

Introduction

Almost all of us have at some time or other come away from an experience and thought that it must be possible to deliver a better service or product. Most of us mutter and grumble a bit, then move on. A smaller number of us continue to develop the idea gently, before gradually moving on from it. What makes the people described in this book different is that they took an idea just like the ones we have had, then they developed it, and then they launched a business based on it which went on to be highly successful.

Which brings me to why we decided, back in 2007, to write the original *How They Started* book, which the following nine stories are taken from. The book, and all the subsequent titles in the How They Started series, was put together for all of you who have had those ideas, whether you have developed them at this stage or not. The collection of nine business stories in this updated *Pocket Edition* of the original has been selected to give you a taste of what we've achieved with the How They Started series, and hopefully whet your appetite for more. We hope, after reading these stories, you're eager to move on to the original *How They Started* book, and its subsequent incarnations: *How They Started: Global Brands*, *How They Started in Tough Times* and the website that inspired the series, Startups.co.uk, where you'll find hundreds more business success stories.

My hope is that the series will both inform and inspire you. Some of you, I hope, will go on to start your own businesses after reading these uplifting tales, and I certainly hope that you will be better prepared for what will happen. But I also hope that some of you will decide, after reading this, that starting your own business is perhaps not for you after all. That should not get in the way of your enjoyment of this, or of your dreaming; perhaps it will be that you simply haven't found the right idea yet.

I have started several businesses myself, which have succeeded, and been involved in or very close to more than a dozen other start-ups, not all of which have made it. I have also seen enough results from venture capitalists who invest in start-ups to know that the chances of new businesses succeeding and thriving are very slim. I know from my own experience that it is both enormously satisfying to create a successful business from scratch, and also extremely hard. To try to get people to buy from your new business in sufficient quantity to make it viable is a real challenge – far harder than to grow something which already exists.

When I first came up with all my new business ideas, many people asked me why, if it was such a good idea, nobody else had done it. It is a really important question, and before you start your own new venture, I suggest that you try to come up with some good answers; try to satisfy yourself, deep down, that you are comfortable that the idea really is good even though no one has done it before. And sleep on it, as my father used to tell me; it is amazing how often you can spot a glaring error in a plan the day after it looked unbeatable!

Interestingly, several people have asked me during the writing of this book whether it has been done before. And indeed, there are one or two books out there which sound as though they might cover the same ground. But they don't. Our entire focus is on how people take an idea and turn it into a business, and the How They Started titles are the first books to go into anything like this much detail about that. I think this is significant – after all, it is that first phase which is the hardest. And of course, blowing my own trumpet for a moment, the series is definitely the only range of titles to be edited by someone who has started several businesses; I hope you will yield the benefit of that in some of the details included.

Let me leave you with one final thought. When we produce our next title in the How They Started series, will we want your new business to be covered?

I hope you enjoy the book.

David Lester
Founder, Startups.co.uk and
Managing Director, Crimson Publishing

Innocent Drinks
Coming to fruition

innocent
little tasty drinks

Founders: Richard Reed, Adam Balon, Jon Wright

Age at start: All 26

Background: The three founders met at university and were engaged in various ventures together there. After working for a number of blue-chip firms they decided to embark on their own business together

Start year: 1999

Business: Fruit juice drinks

Innocent Drinks, which almost single handedly introduced the smoothie to Britain, is now one of the fastest growing drinks brands in Europe, with revenues in excess of £110m. The company, started by three friends, has amazed the business world by successfully launching a preservative-free healthy fruit drink and maintaining its ethical principles, despite its founders having no real experience in the sector. Innocent now employs more than 250 staff and sells to more 13 different countries. The company's offices are among the most friendly and relaxed in the world and its staff are extremely well treated, with perks ranging from free snowboarding trips to bonuses for having children.

Quitting the rat race

Three friends, Richard Reed, Adam Balon and Jon Wright, met at university and often worked on mini-business ventures together. Club nights were a speciality; Richard and Adam organised the nights while Jon designed posters and flyers to attract the crowds. Without realising it, the students were honing promotional skills which would be useful later. Also, they were learning that a sense of fun and enjoyment were important aspects of how they wanted to work. They often talked about running their own company together, although the idea of fruit drinks wasn't to surface until much later.

After university, all three entered the world of big business; Richard worked for advertising agency BMP, Adam went to consultants Bain Associates and Jon worked for management consultants McKinsey and then Virgin. Like so many involved in the 'work hard, play hard' culture of the UK's capital they felt that their diets were far from healthy. At that time, 'juice bars' were opening up in London, offering different blends of fruit, sometimes also involving yoghurt and ice. It struck the three friends that they couldn't be the only ones who wanted something healthy each morning, as they made their way through the arduous commute. They came up with the idea of a healthy drink that could be bought off the shelf, solving the problem they had all experienced of waiting for ages queuing up at a juice bar. Furthermore, they wanted to make something that was totally natural, containing just fruit – no ice or water, let alone preservatives, stabilisers or any other chemical agent.

They began creating their own fruit smoothies at home, and eventually came up with some recipes, which they thought tasted great. Their first was strawberries and bananas, a variety that still sells well today, which was based on a 'communal love of these fruits'. However, with no real experience in making fruit juices or in the soft drinks market, they didn't know whether the product would sell. They knew they needed to do some market research.

In the summer of 1998, the lads decided to open up a smoothie stall at the 'Jazz on the Green' festival in West London that Adam and Richard had been running for a few years. Next to their stall they placed two large empty bins, one marked 'Yes' and the other 'No'. They asked customers to tell them whether or not they should give up their day jobs to start a smoothie business by putting their empty bottles in the appropriate bin. The crowds voted overwhelmingly for them to start a new business, so Jon, Adam and Richard left their jobs.

At this point, they hadn't thought of the name Innocent. While the jazz festival crowds had backed their drinks, they also overwhelmingly

rejected the first trading name of 'Fast Tractor'. Other efforts: Naked, Fresh Inc, Fresh and Thirsty were also discounted before the trio decided upon their name.

'We went through thousands of different names, all the different variations, it was a case of getting the thesaurus out until we came up with Innocent,' Richard says.

The now famous logo was produced by a start-up design agency called Deepend in return for a stake in the business. However, the company went out of business before Innocent went into production, so they never had to give up any of their shares.

Budding innocence

Almost immediately problems beset the plan; there was a massive amount of work to do and the three founders were soon shocked by how tough it could be to set up a new business.

'We were hopelessly naïve,' Richard recalls. 'We stopped working with just a month's pay to keep us going, but it was nine months before we were up and running.'

As with many start-ups, raising money was one of their first major obstacles. They needed to raise money to buy fruit and bottles and get the smoothies made. Bankers and investors were not as easily impressed as the crowds at the festival and shied away from the proposition. There were three overriding factors that the potential investors just couldn't ignore. First, Innocent had no experience in the sector and appeared to have underestimated the complexity of food manufacturing. They had only ever made small quantities of their juices but were looking to expand across the nation. Also, their additive-free healthy offering had a very short shelf life, meaning that unless the product was sold quickly it would go off, which left investors fearing that they might end up owning a lot of rotten fruit.

Finally, it was the late 1990s and the investment world was caught up in a dotcom bubble, which had yet to burst. Everybody was trying to make money out of the internet and nobody was looking to back a fruit juice company. 'I remember hearing about lastminute.com and thinking 'oh my God, that is such a brilliant idea', and for one minute I was thinking "we should do a dotcom",' remembers Richard.

Having left their high-powered jobs behind, the world in which the Innocent founders lived was now a harsh one. 'It was a case of our friends buying us the occasional pint and eating cereal three times a day. We come from great families but they aren't so rich that they could support us to that extent. The business very nearly never happened.'

Straining to succeed

In one final, desperate move Richard sent out an email entitled 'Does anybody know someone rich?' to everyone they had ever known. The email was passed around and, via a former work colleague of Jon, it eventually landed in the inbox of a certain Maurice Pinto.

Pinto was a wealthy American with a lot of experience in investing in new companies. People like this are often referred to as business angels, as they are often the saviours of businesses' ideas, investing money and time to help grow young companies.

Adam, Jon and Richard went to see Maurice and, despite being close to 40 years younger than him, they got along very well. Maurice liked their business plan, and thought that Innocent addressed an important need: he knew that in the US there was a huge demand for smoothies, but the UK still had no real smoothie companies at that stage. The maverick in Maurice also found Innocent's unconventional approach to business refreshing; the trio had high ideals about how the company should behave towards its staff, suppliers and the environment. Maurice was impressed that they didn't rush into decisions and would always debate very heavily before coming to a conclusion, which they had to do because the business has no single leader. Their answer to Maurice's first question, 'who's in charge?' was 'we all are'. In short, Innocent was determined to break the mould in every respect. While this frightened off some investors, in the end Maurice decided to invest £250,000 in return for a 20% stake in the business. Now, the company could really get going.

While they had been looking for funding Innocent had also been attempting to find a manufacturer and this had been no easy process either. 'We went around virtually every drinks manufacturer and they were all saying that we needed to make our smoothies with concentrate. However, we responded by saying that we have tested this and consumers don't want drinks made from concentrate, they want something natural,' Richard says.

Just like with the potential investors, they were turned down again and again. Manufacturers insisted that Innocent needed to use concentrate to make its drinks but the lads knew there was a demand for their natural product. Prior to gaining the funding, they had given small batches of their drinks to shopkeepers for free for them to sell on, as a market test, and the response was overwhelmingly positive.

'The shops wanted to place orders but we had to say "sorry, we're not really ready yet",' Richard recalls.

The quest for a manufacturer eventually brought them to a small family business which agreed to make the drinks the way they wanted, provided that Innocent supply them with the machinery to do the production.

The funding from Maurice came through in early 1999 and Innocent launched later that year with three recipes: strawberries & bananas, cranberries & raspberries and oranges, bananas & pineapples.

To start with Innocent sold its drinks to high-end food retailers such as Harvey Nichols and Harrods, and to what was then a small coffee chain called Café Nero. These were Innocent's 'beacon outlets', though the big retailers were soon to follow. Waitrose was its first supermarket buyer. 'Supermarkets don't even return your calls at first, then they say no and then if you are persistent you get a chance. When we managed to get in front of Waitrose they could appreciate the drink was just right for their audience', Richard says. After Waitrose came Sainsbury's, and shortly after that all the big retailers began stocking their drinks.

From April 1999 until the end of the year, Innocent achieved sales of £400,000. In its second year of trading turnover hit £1.6m, then £4.2m, £6m, £10.6m, £17m, £37m and in 2006, £78m.

The founders were able to draw on their professional experience to set strong foundations for the growth of the company. They made sure that they established strong relationships with suppliers as they viewed them to be vital for their company's success. They also planned ahead and considered where they would be in a year's time.

The company also literally framed its values, which have governed the way it has operated to this day:

- be natural by keeping it human and by using 100% natural fruit all the time;
- be entrepreneurial, chasing opportunities and challenging the status quo;
- be responsible, doing what you believe to be right;
- be commercial, think clearly and act decisively and be generous when offering praise to others and with charitable support.

Where are they now?

All three founders are all still fully involved in the business, which has expanded across Europe. The company now sells over two million smoothies each week in 11,000 outlets. The Innocent range has expanded massively too. The smoothies now come in one litre cartons, and more recently Innocent has branched out into orange juice, and Veg Pots – a range of healthy vegetable-based ready-meals.

In 2009, Innocent controversially sold an 18% stake in the business to Coca-Cola. The deal attracted intense criticism from business and ethical commentators alike who accused the company of abandoning its 'innocent' image by selling to a multinational corporation. However, the three founders defended the decision, insisting that altruistic aims were still at the heart of the business – even today 10% of all profits are given to the Innocent Foundation, which funds NGOs in countries from where the fruit for the smoothies is sourced. In 2010 Maurice Pinto sold all his shares in the company as part of a further deal which saw Coca-Cola become a majority shareholder in Innocent.

Bravissimo
A personal solution
for a large market

Founder: **Sarah Tremellen**

Age at start: **28**

Background: **TV/radio marketing**

Start year: **1995**

Business: **Lingerie, swimwear and clothing retailer**

L ike many great new business ideas, Sarah Tremellen's Bravissimo began life as a solution to a problem. When Sarah fell pregnant in 1993, she discovered there was a shortage of attractive lingerie for women whose bust size was larger than a D-cup; this very personal story has clearly had much public resonance as over a million women have contacted the business since Bravissimo was launched in 1995. By 2010 the company reached the £45m turnover mark, a growth which has been steady since its earliest years and has made Bravissimo one of the UK's fastest growing companies.

Solving a big problem

According to Sarah, who went up six bust cup sizes during her pregnancy, the idea for Bravissimo was first conceived during a discussion with a friend who had also experienced difficulties buying larger sized bras. They realised that their plight was not unusual and yet the high street failed to offer women like them an attractive range of lingerie in any one place. As Sarah explains, high-street stockists have to offer a variety of styles to their customers, so they tend to stock this large range of styles only in cup sizes A–D to suit their assumed customer-type. They are therefore only able to stock two or three 'big cup styles' to suit customers with a larger bust.

This situation meant that large-busted women would enter a shop and see a range of bras they couldn't fit into and so would often have to ask the shop assistants which styles were available in their size, an awkward thing to do for many women. This meant that even if the bra they eventually left the store with was wonderful, the experience of buying it had been nonetheless 'demoralising'.

13

Sarah understood this and her aim, therefore, was to create a lingerie mail-order company which specialised in larger bust sizes, where 'everything was provided under one roof', and at the same time to create a 'forum' where big-breasted women could not only feel comfortable with their figures but could celebrate their size.

Sarah's first idea was to open a shop in the vein of those she thought so conspicuously absent on the high street. But she soon realised that she could not afford to purchase the amount of stock she would need to fill a shop and it became clear that a mail-order business would suit her financial restrictions better, since she would only need to place orders for goods once customers had ordered from her. This quickly became a more viable option as Sarah realised she could start the mail-order business from home, which was also a convenient starting place for a new mother.

At the start of her pregnancy, Sarah and her husband had organised their finances to account for the fact that Sarah would not be working and would become a full-time mum, and therefore there would be only one income coming in. As a result of this planning, Sarah was able to spend a reasonable amount of time investigating her business idea – a key stage in setting up a new business – without the pressure of having to earn a living.

Sarah set about her initial research by enquiring in high-street stores, writing to fashion magazines and reading market research reports in libraries. While doing this she also discovered that there was a government scheme which offered a £60 weekly enterprise allowance to people starting up new businesses, in exchange for compulsory attendance at a weekly evening business course which would run for eight weeks. Knowing that the money would come in handy and that

the information could be valuable, Sarah signed up almost immediately, merging her small allowance into her standard account and spending her time learning about key start-up issues such as how to register for VAT and self-employed income tax. At the end of the course each student was expected to show what they had learnt, presenting a business plan to the head of the course. Sarah excelled in this, using it as a chance to offer a prototype of her product. At the end of her presentation a bank manger, who happened to be sitting on the panel for her course's presentations, told her that she really liked the idea, and offered her a £10,000 loan on the proviso that Sarah and her friend, who was now to become her business partner, invested £3,000 each. They accepted, and the business was established.

At the time, Sarah's husband was working for Tetley Tea as a planning manager and he sensibly informed her that in order to run a mail-order company she would need a database. Admitting that it 'hadn't even occurred' to her, she accepted his offer to write one for her – despite his lack of experience in the field.

As it turns out, it was a wise move. After three months labouring over the computer system a primitive version was ready; and a more complete one followed a few months later that was used for the next seven years. Tailor made to suit exactly Bravissimo's needs, Sarah recalls it was a wonderful thing, as if she wanted the system to do something different she had only to ask her husband to make the amendments. The only downside, she adds, was that the company became dependent on one person. Today, it has an IT department!

Forced to think laterally

This was just the beginning, and the journey ahead was by no means smooth. It was at this early stage, while the company was still being set up, that Sarah ran into her first major problem.

Just four miles down the road another mail-order company – which also had a shop – was already in operation, and was buying bras from the same manufacturers that Sarah and her partner had begun to approach. Despite the fact that Bravissimo was at that time only a mail-order company, the other company objected to Sarah's business setting up in such close proximity and decided to contact many of the large bra manufacturers to try and dissuade them from supplying Bravissimo.

This company was a well-established brand and therefore had enough influence to convince the manufacturers that supplying Bravissimo would be a bad idea.

Only a few days before the other business began to intervene, Sarah had been to a trade show in Birmingham and had approached several manufacturers who she says had been 'really positive'. However, a few days following this show these manufactures started to contact Sarah to withdraw their support. Sarah later found out that this was a direct result of the other business contacting the manufacturers and persuading them that supplying Bravissimo would affect their established business relationship. Sarah points out that the bra manufacturers' sales representatives worked on commission, and so were keener to continue to deal with a secure, established brand rather than risk dealing with her, a brand new business with no experience in the sector.

Sarah recalls that it was at this point she became 'really determined', citing this 'horrendous' experience coupled with her first-time experience of motherhood as the fuel which spurred her on. Echoing the mantra of self-belief so necessary for those starting up a business, she describes how this convinced her for 'the first time ever' to stick with something and to make a success of all her hard work.

At first Sarah tried 'begging and pleading' with the manufacturers, only to be told that they absolutely would not supply her. Resolute, Sarah reconsidered her approach and remembered an article she had read at her university careers centre which suggested that many people who rang up companies asking for a job were immediately told 'no', but those that rang up asking for advice were often able to be seen and consequently might 'get through the door'. So with this in mind, Sarah decided that she would approach the manufactures simply to 'talk' to them about their market. By doing so she was able to retain contact with them while she considered what other options were open to her.

Sarah briefly considered the idea of manufacturing her own bras but says this was never really what she wanted to do. 'We weren't bra designers, we wanted to deal with the public', she says. It was in autumn 1994 that she decided instead to devise what she refers to as a 'cheesy marketing document' to persuade manufacturers that they were making a big mistake in not supplying Bravissimo – that if they did not supply Bravissimo they would be missing a fantastic opportunity.

This 'cheesy marketing document' turned out to be one of the best things to happen to the new business, forcing Sarah 'to think about what her business was really about' and ultimately leading to the creation of Bravissimo as a more wholly marketed brand which celebrated the full-bodied figure. During this marketing planning process, Sarah came up with the idea of producing a 'magazine' which exceeded the scope of traditional bra catalogues by including articles and letters about large-busted women.

Sarah outsourced the design of the magazine to a friend of a friend who was just starting up herself and therefore offered them a 'cheap deal'. Once the outline of this was in place, Sarah approached Honor Blackman – who was also a friend of a friend – to feature in the magazine, something she was 'only too happy to do'. Sarah points out that there often seems to be a common desire among the famous to 'champion the underdog' and it is therefore worth approaching such people through any tenuous link.

And so it became this combination of articles, features and photos in its mail-order catalogue that set Bravissimo apart as a brand and ended up being its saving grace. The idea went down so well that the three manufacturers Sarah showed it to all agreed to supply Bravissimo. In addition, they agreed to supply promotional pictures of the merchandise for the first published magazine – saving Sarah money on production costs. Sarah's dream was starting to come to life.

While her primary aim had been to convince manufacturers that Bravissimo was an opportunity not to be missed, Sarah still had to overcome the problem of the rival company. This she did by creating the perception that Bravissimo was an Oxford-based company, and was no longer in London, since the problem the competitor had was its location in the near vicinity. Sarah decided to create a 'virtual office' at her parents' house in Oxford, where she set up a PO box and an Oxford telephone number which was on permanent divert to London. She was very careful never to let on publicly that Bravissimo was not an Oxford-based company. As part of this she would drive to Oxford twice a week to collect items – an extreme measure, but according to Sarah all this was necessary as a means of allowing the company to focus on making itself a positive brand rather than the victim of a competitor's negative campaign. This focus is still important to her and has since been incorporated into her business practice, as she states, 'I want people to shop with us, whatever the competition, because they want to shop with us, not because we stop them shopping elsewhere.'

The rival company eventually discovered, via a mutual contact, that Bravissimo was still based in London. However, by this time its attempts to thwart Sarah's efforts were unsuccessful. Sarah had by now produced the magazine and was buying stock from the manufacturers, who now had faith in Bravissimo succeeding. The competitor's attempts to rid itself of Bravissimo's competition only resulted in its increasing unpopularity, and four years later this rival company disbanded after expanding too quickly and running into cashflow problems. In a suitable twist of fate, Sarah managed to buy its mail-order list from the receivers; as she says, 'so often in life, what goes around, comes around'.

Having won support from three bra manufacturers and with a finished magazine, Sarah was finally in a position to launch Bravissimo. This she did in January 1995. Now, looking back, she admits that at this time she was naïve and inexperienced and working with only 'a bit of common sense and gut feeling'.

Together with a few friends and her husband, she created a database with just 75 people as target customers. These names were a combination of friends, family and people she had encountered when conducting her research or attending trade shows. Sarah explains that one major benefit of starting with such a small base was that it allowed her to 'evolve, develop and learn' without making mistakes that impacted the business negatively. While most businesses have to rely on other people's expertise, she says she was able to 'take time and work on a trial and error basis' and so deepen her understanding of the business.

Three days after sending out the first catalogue and magazine, Bravissimo made its first sale – albeit from Sarah's business partner's mother-in-law! Over the next three weeks approximately 150 people registered on the mailing list and around 30 bras were sold. However, after three weeks Sarah had an 'enormous dose of luck' which would really get Bravissimo off the ground.

As part of her 'launch plan' for the business, Sarah had sent a number of the first 5,000 copies of Bravissimo's magazine to various newspapers and women's magazines such as *Good Housekeeping* and *She*. It struck a chord with a journalist from *Femail*, the women's section of the *Daily Mail*, and the result was a double-page spread in a

Wednesday edition of the newspaper. This feature led to an explosion of interest and in the three days following the article, Bravissimo received a staggering 1,500 calls. This surge continued for some time so that, by the end of that first year, there were 11,000 women registered on the database and Bravissimo had sold £134,000 of underwear.

Sarah and her business partner hired their first member of staff in the summer of 1995 and another before December of that year, along with some temps to assist with the administrative work – one of who remained with the company and eventually became Bravissimo's product director. Sarah explains that the people she hired were often not particularly interested in the fashion business, but she had difficulty recruiting those who were, since they were not interested in working with two women, new to the industry, who were working from a sitting room! Furthermore, as the company continued to grow at a pace (turnover for the second year was £400,000) there was little time for a long, formal recruitment process and help was often taken where offered. With hindsight, Sarah now warns of the importance of adequate delegation, saying that as the company grew during its second year so many people were hired to do relatively menial tasks that they became something of an 'amorphous mass'.

Eventually, Sarah and her business partner decided instead to train people to do specific jobs and delegate responsibilities accordingly. Over the last 15 years Sarah has granted more and more of her own responsibilities to the strong team which now surrounds her.

Although Bravissimo's turnover has grown steadily since its launch (currently in excess of £45m), the business did not make a profit until the summer of 1998. By this time Sarah had bought her partner out of the business. Unusually, the lack of profits early on did not cause problems due to the nature of the company's positive cashflow; as a mail-order company Bravissimo bought goods from suppliers once it had received orders from customers. The customers paid up front, but Bravissimo had arranged six week terms with its suppliers so Sarah could use new customers' cash to pay for last month's goods. This meant that even though on paper Bravissimo was not making a profit, there was always money in the bank and the company was able to break even in cash terms for the first three years without having to take out any outside loans.

Sarah was not fazed by not seeing any profit in the early years. She says that her focus was elsewhere. 'I loved the idea of setting up a business because I loved creating something and developing it and watching it growing bigger. It didn't bother me that I wasn't being paid – although if it had gone on for 11 years, then I might not have been so content!'.

Where are they now?

Sarah Tremellen is still very much involved with Bravissimo today. After running the business under her sole ownership for three and a half years following the departure of her partner, she was eventually joined by her husband. They now run the company together.

Since opening its first shop, to sit alongside its online and mail-order service, the company's retail presence has gone from strength to strength. At the time of writing there are 20 stores open across the UK, with plans to open more. Having celebrated its 15th birthday in 2010, the lingerie company continues to grow, and managed to increase its turnover and record healthy profit margins throughout the recession.

Glasses Direct
A clear vision

GLASSESDIRECT.CO.UK®

Founder: James Murray-Wells

Age at start: 21

Background: Student

Start year: 2004

Business: Online glasses retailer

G lasses Direct has probably had more column inches in the national press over the last few years than any other business in this book. Its impressive press coverage is due to the fact that one man decided to take on an entire industry, and seems to be winning. It is a story of justice and triumph of 'the little guy' over corporate giants, made all the more appealing by the fact that its founder was a student when he set up the business, which is now selling millions of pounds worth of glasses every year.

Shocked into action

James Murray-Wells was just 21 when the idea for Glasses Direct came to him, studying English at the University of the West of England, Bristol. Despite his youth, James already had a keen business mind and had been looking for business opportunities for years when he came up with the idea for Glasses Direct. He was adept at IT and had developed an interest in 'the way the internet was heading'; he confesses that he saw university as a good time to look out for business ideas that might work online. 'As universities generally (and English degrees in particular!) bought with them a lot of free time as well as good support networks, they provide a great launch pad for starting a business,' explains James.

One day he learned that he needed reading glasses for the first time (which he puts down to too much reading, primarily Harry Potter) and was shocked by how expensive glasses were. Even the frames alone often cost over £100, while the total price of a pair of glasses could easily reach several hundred pounds. Realising that the high-street prices simply had to be too much money for what was essentially 'some wire and some glass', James felt sure that there must be a dramatic mark up on the manufacturers cost to the opticians, which meant that a web-based business could offer customers a much better deal and still make good money.

So James started work researching the manufacturing costs of a pair of glasses. Trawling internet forums and chatting online to people in the trade, he also took advantage of the university's late-night library facilities. Here, he spent time looking in the *Yellow Pages* for manufacturers' contact numbers and then rang them up, picking their brains about the different parts of the process and asking if he could stop by and see for himself.

He soon learned that he had indeed been right, and that the high-street opticians were making enormous profit margins on the spectacles they were selling. So he decided to go for it, and set up a website to sell glasses to the public.

His first task was to find some suppliers to make glasses for him. The manufacturers he contacted were mainly helpful and after a few visits, James chose some that he wanted to buy from. But after their initial helpfulness, it proved very difficult for James to persuade them to supply him. Being only 21 and with no business background, most manufacturers were extremely reluctant to open an account with Glasses Direct. It did not help that his whole premise was essentially trying to take business away from the manufacturers' major customers, the high-street opticians. Nonetheless, after much hard work and a fair amount of rejection, James found a few manufacturers happy to work with him, and he agreed terms with them.

As a test, he arranged to forward his own prescription on to the manufacturer, who would then send him a pair of glasses with the

correct lenses in. The test worked. When the glasses arrived at his house a few weeks later, at a cost of just £6, it was the moment, he says, when he first thought, 'this will work'.

James planned to focus his new business on supplying glasses to people with prescriptions, unlike most opticians which carry out eye tests for customers and then supply them with glasses or contact lenses afterwards. He called it Glasses Direct, to make it crystal clear what the business was about, and so that search engines would

27

find it more easily when potential customers searched for glasses or spectacles.

There were two major hurdles for customers buying glasses from a website. The first was the need to get a prescription – people weren't used to getting their eyes tested and walking out of a shop with the prescription without ordering any glasses. Second, glasses can obviously make a significant difference to people's image, and most customers spend ages trying on different pairs in opticians' shops. Clearly they can't do that physically when buying from a website. While this is also true for clothes, it is easy for people buying clothes by mail order to send them back if they aren't quite right – but because each pair of glasses is made specially for a customer, with lenses cut to fit each set of frames, most high-street opticians don't let customers simply return them if they don't like the way they look.

James thought about how to get over these issues; if he couldn't, his business wouldn't work. He thought that by offering substantial savings over high-street prices, he would be able to persuade enough customers to walk out with their prescriptions and try buying online. He also came up with an idea for a tool on the website which lets customers try the frames on virtually using a digital photo of themselves, so they can see what they would look like in each pair before ordering. In fact, this probably works better than the high-street shops, since most people can't see themselves properly in a new set of frames, not having the appropriate lenses in at that stage. And just to make sure people would feel comfortable buying from the web, James bravely decided to offer a full no quibble refund policy to anyone who wasn't happy with their glasses.

Moving swiftly

The next step was to design the website. James started developing this himself while he was still studying for his finals, and finished it in the summer holidays when a friend who was studying design at university came over to James' parents' house to help him out. James went to pick him up from the station and drove him to the house and back, day-in-day-out, until the website began to take serious shape in early July. The process itself, though hard work, was at least reasonably cheap. As James says, the beauty of an e-business is that one is able to get it up and running quite cheaply; in his case, using the last instalment of his student loan.

All James really needed was his website, and relationships with other suppliers. He managed to get his manufacturers to hold the stock (of frames) for him, and then dispatch the finished glasses directly to the customers, whose addresses Glasses Direct would supply. As a result, James' young company could start doing business without opening its own warehouse or taking on staff. So once this was in place, James concentrated on getting the website ready to go live, after registering the company with the Medicines and Healthcare products Regulatory Agency on 1st July 2004.

Not surprisingly, given the brand new concept and no publicity, the website wasn't an immediate success, with sales in the first month averaging one or two pairs a day. But this proved to be the quintessential calm before the storm.

James knew he had to tell people that his new business existed but he didn't have a huge marketing budget to do this with. He decided to print some leaflets promoting Glasses Direct, and roped in some friends

29

to help him hand them out to potential customers. He recalls getting on a train at Bristol Temple Meads station and handing out flyers all the way down the train 'so people would have to sit, stuck, with our flyers to read for the whole journey'. It was an advertising manoeuvre that clearly worked: the website statistics showed that many people had logged on to the site when reaching such destinations as Bristol International Airport!

As well as this, word was gradually spreading, boosted by happy customers telling their friends. According to James, people were so used to paying £150 for a pair of glasses that they were amazed to see the same deal elsewhere for £15 – especially the early customers who had placed orders when they were not really sure whether to trust this website or not, and received glasses that were as good as the expensive high-street models. Consequently, the rate of orders coming in every day grew rapidly; an average day during August that year saw 100 pairs ordered. Thank-you letters started to arrive too, something that James proudly points to as a real distinguishing feature for his company as compared to the big chains.

He was also lucky, he says, in that his business was very cashflow positive from the early days. Customers would pay by debit or credit card with their order, and Glasses Direct wouldn't need to pay suppliers until 30 days later, which meant that its bank account grew rapidly from its revenues, which is not normally the case with many start-up businesses. In addition to this the young business had very low overheads to start with, another thing in its favour as a start-up venture.

Luckily for James, his business continued growing at the same fast pace. After renting some nearby office space within a month of starting the business, he also took on his first 'official' member of staff – someone to manage finances and, as he puts it, 'put us on the straight and narrow' and help get things in order; despite being a web-based business, the paperwork from the high volume of orders was enormous, and needed to be filed and monitored properly.

Meanwhile, James was busy trying to drum up publicity for his new business. He wrote to lots of journalists he thought might be interested in the Glasses Direct story, asking them to write about him. In August, the media started to pick up his story, in particular an article in the *Daily Telegraph*. 'This gave the business a massive boost,' James says, as he advises new companies with a 'genuine hook or interesting story' to persevere with getting some strong media coverage; James thinks it's the best way to get a business going.

With such a successful start and great PR, the story sounds like it must have been plain sailing from here on. But it wasn't. James faced significant opposition from the high-street competitors and says that this was Glasses Direct's biggest hurdle. He claims that 'the industry hates us', and he points to a variety of challenges and legal threats to prove his point. However, he goes on to add that in fact the competition has only made the company stronger. The British press love stories of underdogs taking on established corporate giants, and James' personal charm and startling story about the true costs of glasses proved irresistible, leading to lots more high profile articles about Glasses Direct being picked on by the high-street opticians. James also admits that these difficulties have only made him stronger, unwilling to stand by and be beaten.

A happy ending

In the first 18 months of business, Glasses Direct generated sales of £1.5m – a tremendous achievement for a new business started by someone straight out of university. James has invested heavily to make sure that Glasses Direct continues to grow; rather than taking money generated from profits out of the business, every penny during the early years was pumped back into the venture.

James decided to take on outside investors towards the end of 2004, and in 2009 took on his biggest funding round to date – £10m. He was keen to build up the company's credibility and provide ever better service to the customer. There is little doubt that having the backing of registered opticians, as the business has now, has strengthened the company's reputation and helped ensure its growth, with turnover figures at the last count hitting the £10m mark.

With plans for the future revolving around international expansion – with particular focus on the United States – James recommends that anyone thinking of starting up a web business should 'think global from the beginning'. To start too focused on one country and then attempt to expand later only prolongs the inevitable and means you have to play 'catch-up' with the rest of the world when they jump on your bandwagon. James is convinced, with the benefit of hindsight, that if the Glasses Direct website had been launched simultaneously for multiple countries, the company would by now be well on its way to saturating not just the UK market but a global one.

Where are they now?

Still working hard to ensure Glasses Direct becomes a household name worldwide, James Murray-Wells has received numerous entrepreneurial awards since starting up the company in 2004, including the UK's most prestigious award for new businesses, Startups.co.uk's Startup Business of the Year gong in 2005. In 2009 the company secured £10m investment from Index Ventures, Highland Capital and Acton Capital Partners.

2010 saw the launch of the company's sister site, Hearingdirect.com, which took the same principle of the original business and applied it to the hearing aid market, with prices starting at £99.

PizzaExpress
Inspired by Italy

Founder: Peter Boizot

Age at start: 35

Background: Sales, teaching, journalism and street selling

Start year: 1965

Business: Pizzeria

PizzaExpress is sufficiently well known that it needs almost no introduction. Today it operates 376 pizza restaurants in the UK and Europe, and has made several entrepreneurs justly successful and famous. In 1965 when Peter Boizot opened the first ever PizzaExpress, its future was much harder to predict.

Peter returned home from a stint working and travelling in Italy but couldn't find even a slice of pizza anywhere in England, let alone a pizzeria. Convinced of the potential, he swiftly set about changing that.

Culinary inspiration

Peter's taste buds first sampled pizza in 1948 when his headmaster dispatched him, aged 18, on a three-month foreign exchange programme to experience life with the Uzielli de Mari family, in Forte deiMarmi near Pisa, Tuscany.

Pizza was a favourite in the Uzielli de Mari household and soon became equally admired by its enthusiastic guest. Peter, repulsed by blood and the slaughter of animals, at the age of five had turned vegetarian and had subsequently grown up on a bland variation of the British staple of meat and boiled veg, minus the meat. Discovering pizza was a revelation.

In Peter's *The PizzaExpress Cookbook*, written in 1976 (Penguin Group Ltd), the founder recalls, 'It was colourful to look at, fragrant to smell, succulent to taste. As a non-meat eater, to eat a pizza with mozzarella with tomato on a pastry base with an olive or two was just up my street. The pizza became, from that moment, a food which was to nurture my body and my pocket for many years to come.'

After completing his National Service in Egypt and studying history at Cambridge University, in 1953 Peter seized the opportunity to live abroad again. A short spell teaching in Paris was followed by a period working for Nestlé in Switzerland, while a move into sales took him to Germany and on visits across much of Europe before he made his way back to Italy and its capital, Rome.

Here, Peter first showed his entrepreneurial flair, which he insists was always part of his genetic make-up, combining work as a journalist for the Associated Press with selling souvenirs and postcards to tourists from a barrow in St Peter's in Vincoli Square. Long, tiring but enjoyable days were rewarded with heady nights of pizza and wine. Peter was in heaven.

Deciding to go it alone

Eventually the pull of home and the nagging conscience to pursue a career took him back to England, but he was determined not to leave his love for pizza in Italy for a second time – or at least that was the plan.

'Back in England, I just couldn't find a pizza – not even the Italian restaurants did them,' he insists. Driven by a yearning to live life as an individual and by a reluctance to work for someone else, Peter decided to solve this problem himself.

'Sick of them not existing I thought "why don't I open my own place?" So in 1965, that's what I did.'

Starting up

Peter's mantra was authenticity. He wanted to make, sell and, yes, eat real Italian pizza, albeit made in the UK.

The first job was to buy a proper Italian pizza oven – and there was only one place to start. 'I flew to the home of pizza, Naples, got in a cab and said "take me to your local pizzeria",' recalls Peter. 'There I was sent to meet Signor Notaro, a manufacturer of ovens, who agreed, for £600, which was a lot of money back then, to send it to England along with an Italian chef to work it.'

Aside from an authentic oven, the other 'essential' was real mozzarella. Shipping from Italy every week in the 1960s was unrealistic, but Peter tracked down London's only mozzarella producer and agreed a deal for exclusive supply – and a whole lot more than he'd originally bargained for. The deal didn't just secure Peter an unrivalled cheese supply, but also the now great PizzaExpress name and his first premises.

The mozzarella factory was owned by Margaret Zampi, widow of the late film director Mario Zampi, who several years before his death had unsuccessfully tried to launch a pizza restaurant, named PizzaExpress, on Wardour Street in London's Soho.

'He'd done everything properly. It was the ideal setting, he imported an oven, even set up a cheese factory,' says Peter. 'However, movie stars craved more luxurious food and unfortunately Zampi, with his simple pizza, was ahead of his time.'

Zampi eventually caved in, undertook an expensive refurbishment, changed the name to The Romanella and began offering standard Italian fare. Despite initial success, The Romanella had fallen on hard times following Zampi's death and was on the verge of liquidation. Peter saw it as an opportunity, however, so he borrowed £100 from a friend, Renee, and made an offer to acquire the ailing company from the widow.

'She was most helpful and she agreed to sell me the shares of PizzaExpress Ltd,' says Peter in his much loved cookbook. It's since proved a fine investment of course, but at the time, he wasn't so sure. 'I took on the staggering task of repaying creditors £14,000. It seemed a lunatic deal,' he admits.

Pursuing the Italian vision

Despite securing the keys to 29 Wardour Street, a prime location at the centre of London's nightlife and dining, it was to be months before Peter opened. In a decision he was later to at least partly reverse, Peter decided there was no need for the plush décor of The Romanella in a modern pizzeria and set about ripping it all out. However, with insufficient tools and labour, or money to pay for either, it proved a frustrating and turbulent process.

To make matters worse, Peter's one tonne Italian oven made it across Europe and over the Channel but was never going to fit through the front door, forcing them to knock down a sidewall to accommodate it. Confused at holding paintbrushes instead of spinning dough, Peter's Italian manager left and his imported chef handed in his notice. Peter had to act fast, and swiftly found chef Rino Silvestri, from Naples, to step in.

When the first PizzaExpress eventually opened its doors, trade was slow. 'Only people who had been to Italy had tried pizza and it was obvious my idea was not properly understood by the denizens of Soho,' he says. 'We started by cutting large pizzas into eight slices and giving them away on grease-proof paper through the front window. People loved it and would walk by shouting, "Ahh, pizza pizza!" but when we started to charge (at two shillings (10p) a slice), business began to wane.'

Peter was fiercely determined to persevere and rejected calls by onlookers and well-meaning advisors to supplement his menu with more familiar British favourites, such as chips and sandwiches. He opened before lunch and didn't close until four or five in the morning, picking up trade from the late night drinkers who stopped by for a slice.

Adapting the business plan

While he flatly refused to compromise on his pure pizza vision, eventually Peter was persuaded to revise his business plan. Ronald Simpson, a friend from Cambridge and City banker Peter had turned to for investment, suggested they move slightly up market.

'I had this romantic rustica idea of selling everyday-life Italian food served up on grease-proof paper or paper plates. However, it's a difficult

41

economic base to grow from as people stay a long time and spend little. We didn't have a nice enough décor to attract higher reaches of Soho, so Simpson suggested we should trade up a little.' Together with Simpson, Peter was able to raise enough money for this improvement.

For the redesign, Peter turned to Italian designer Enzo Apicella, who, ironically, had fitted out The Romanella Peter had ripped apart. Later Enzo worked on 85 PizzaExpress restaurants and was responsible for designing its famous art nouveau logo and 'PizzaPizzaPizza' window pattern. In came a wine menu, dining tables and simple but attractive furnishings – the first restaurant to resemble the format we all now know and love.

The upgrade drew in Soho's diners and pizza quickly became more than a mere street snack. Overcoming one further obstacle of seeing off a neighbouring competitor and eventually acquiring it, Peter embraced the attention of becoming London's latest culinary hotspot, using his status as host to entertain press and cement his reputation as something of a local celebrity and to get PizzaExpress known to the masses.

Express expansion

Within three or four months, the relaunched PizzaExpress was bringing in a healthy £2,000–£3,000 a week in sales. Peter is proud to have brought over the first Peroni beers from Italy, as he approached the manufacturer in Naples and asked to sell it in his pizzeria in England.

A second restaurant followed 18 months later in a former dairy factory on Bloomsbury's Coptic Street next to the British Museum. Peter says that this step is never easy for any business, but the company adjusted and expanded accordingly. Enzo again designed it with a remit to replicate the aura of the first PizzaExpress but with a completely unique design and décor.

This became a feature of PizzaExpress' roll-out, with Peter as determined to avoid becoming a homogenous and faceless chain as he was to grow the business. His first ambition was not to create the chain that PizzaExpress is today, but to succeed at one or two restaurants at a time, although he admits it had occurred to him that the concept may well grow.

'I always loathed the idea of a chain,' he says. 'It's well documented that I saw the PizzaExpress company as a necklace with each restaurant being an individual and unique gem. Each time we opened a restaurant we added a gem.'

The Coptic Street restaurant was the first to feature original artwork on the walls and live jazz, something which, along with the deliberate sourcing of unusual and unique buildings, continues to set both PizzaExpress and its individual restaurants apart.

The first two years of PizzaExpress also saw Peter introduce his personal invention, the Pizza Veneziana, to the menu, with a percentage of every one sold going to the 'Venice in Peril Fund'. More than £1m has since been raised and Peter has been formally honoured by the Italian government by way of thanks, as well as receiving an MBE at home.

Roll-out

Expansion followed steadily and then rapidly throughout the '70s, '80s and early '90s through traditional roll-out and briefly a franchising model, as the nation quickly developed a hunger for a food unknown to its shores just decades before. For most of this time, the business was generating more cash than it needed to grow, so little extra finance was required. Peter acknowledges, though, that he was fortunate to have a 'generally helpful bank' and that his original investor Simpson remained an active investor for many years.

The opening of the 50th PizzaExpress restaurant on South King Street in Manchester in the 1980s stands out to Peter as his proudest moment. 'It felt like a real achievement,' he says. 'Like we'd finally become a big company.'

Peter eventually sold his shares to the PizzaExpress company in 1993, a group consisting of David Page's G+F holdings, Star Computers (a front company for Luke Johnson and Hugh Osmond) and Matthew Allen. Since then the company has been floated on the stock exchange, taken private again, and made fortunes for the three now well-known entrepreneurs, Johnson, Osmond and Page. The company is currently owned by Gondola Holdings which also owns the ASK, Zizzi and Bryron restaurant chains. However, PizzaExpress remains the market leader with 376 restaurants

Peter believes the one thing that made PizzaExpress work is what keeps it successful today: authentic Italian pizza. In the foreword to *The PizzaExpress Cookbook*, he quips: 'Those who have sought to change the original Italian images of the pizza receive my condolences for not being able to think of a name for their products, because it sure isn't pizza the way God intended it!'

Entrepreneurial vision

Looking back even to the earliest days of struggle and sale by the slice, Peter is adamant he never doubted the potential of pizza or that he was the man to introduce it to the UK public's palates.

'The world was my oyster! I believed I could go as far as I could,' he insists. 'I liked doing my own thing and so took well to being my own boss. I don't regret anything, and wouldn't change a thing.'

Where are they now?

Peter Boizot has since gone on to own other businesses, including restaurants, hotels, retail property and Peterborough United Football Club, as well as becoming heavily involved in the jazz scene, starting the Soho Jazz Festival. He also played hockey competitively until into his late 60s! Now, in his 80s, he's just as passionate about life, business and PizzaExpress as ever.

Today, PizzaExpress also has a retail arm, which provides ready-made versions of its pizzas to supermarkets across the country. In fact, it sells as many pizzas in supermarkets as it does in its restaurants.

moneysupermarket.com
A wealth of experience

moneysupermarket.com®
the price comparison site

Founder: Simon Nixon

Age at start: 32

Background: Mortgage broker

Start year: 1999

Business: Price comparison website

n 1999, the UK's first personal finance price comparison site for consumers was launched by mortgage broker Simon Nixon. moneysupermarket.com provided a wealth of information and aimed from the outset to be a 'consumer champion'. The group's websites, including the original site and travelsupermarket.com, are now visited by more than 120 million people a year and, although the web has been flooded with replicas, moneysupermarket.com retains its position as the UK's leading financial comparison site. Simon began with a solid background in providing accessible mortgage information, which he was able to adapt to his new venture. He was also able to use an existing business model to make moneysupermarket.com's creation relatively painless.

An entrepreneurial mind

This extraordinary story starts in 1989 when Simon dropped out of a much-hated finance and accountancy degree at Nottingham University in his first year; he had no idea which career path to pursue, much to the distress of his parents. They presented him with the job section in their local newspaper, the *Chester Chronicle*, and 'basically forced' him to apply for the first post he was vaguely suited to, which turned out to be a position as a financial consultant. Simon warmed to the idea of 'making some money', but aged only 20, he felt disinclined to sell life insurance and pensions. Following this logic, he decided to specialise in the more relevant area of mortgages. He quickly found that 'the harder you work and the more innovative you are, the more money you make', as he was effectively self-employed, working on a commission-only basis.

How They Started

Simon realised that if he teamed up with a local sales office, he may be able to get sales representatives to contact him directly to set up mortgages for their clients. He approached the nearby Chester Persimmon Homes office and asked if his services would aid their sales, quickly discovering that one in two people wanting to buy homes from them could not as they had been refused mortgages. Simon made himself the first port of call for this sales office and started getting five or six mortgage enquiries a day. Soon, having only been working for a few months, he was the top salesperson in his office. The managing director of Persimmon Homes then asked him to provide information for three or four of their other offices. Simon describes how 'all of a sudden, I had someone helping me arrange mortgages'. This experience gave Simon a taste for the success of ingenuity. He also spotted an opportunity: there was no resource in the market for financial advisors like himself to find the best mortgage for their customer.

Realising this, Simon bought an Apple Mac computer and in his spare time put together a fortnightly trade magazine, *Brokers Update*, listing the best deals and every product for reference. He initially sent out 500 free copies and charged £11 per month on standing order, with the first month free. Simon recalls that for every 100 copies he sent out, he received 10 standing orders. It was so successful that within three or four months he was making more money from magazine subscription than from arranging mortgages.

Simon recognised he had to focus on either the magazine or mortgage brokering and decided to pursue the magazine as he thought it had more potential and found it more interesting. He recruited two people to work with him, bought a printing press from his savings and leaped into the world of publishing.

The magazine performed well but within two years, subscriptions started to plateau as mortgage brokers began relying more on computer technology. Information could be accessed immediately, so the magazine was already a couple of days out of date by the time it landed on their desk; something had to change. Simon, innovative as always, used funds saved from his magazine and began writing a software package that was updated daily over the internet, allowing brokers to enter criteria and find the most competitive mortgage. He was joined by software programmer and business partner Duncan Cameron, who Simon eventually bought out of the company. Mortgage 2000 launched in 1994 and Simon estimates that this software is currently used by about 40% of all mortgage brokers in Britain. He acknowledges that had he just kept the magazine going, it probably would have died a few years later and he emphasises the need to keep 'spotting opportunities' and 'move with the times'.

To house his business venture, Simon initially rented a room in the Chester Enterprise Centre, where they helped new businesses get on their feet. Eventually he was able to buy a terraced house in the Hoole district of Chester where the business stayed until 1998, when the company purchased its first purpose built office on the then new Chester Business Park. The company is still run from a Chester HQ to this day.

Breakthrough

Simon's 'real break' came in 1999 when Freeserve introduced free access to the internet. He envisaged creating a site that used the information from Mortgage 2000 but changed the interface so that consumers themselves could use it. Simon also decided to broaden the information they could access to include other areas of personal finance, such as loans and credit cards to create a price comparison site.

Extending research to other areas was easy: with a solid background in mortgages and having produced financial information for several years now, the transition was 'bread and butter to us'. Simon took on more researchers who specialised in personal finance, recruited internet developers and purchased some servers. He feels it is important to have an in-depth knowledge of the business you are dealing in. While some entrepreneurs will jump into a market they think will be lucrative, Simon warns that without sound prior knowledge, there is a greater chance that the business will not be successful.

It was while setting up Mortgage 2000 that Simon went through the hard process of establishing a business from scratch, not in his second venture – he warns that 'in business, if you work really hard, you take two steps forward and one step back'. Therefore, moneysupermarket.com was able to lean on Mortgage 2000 and benefit from its legal and administrative infrastructure and personnel, of which there were 40 or 50 by this point.

In total, Simon estimates that moneysupermarket.com cost around £100,000 to set up, most of which was spent on PR, and because of Mortgage 2000's success, the new venture already had cash reserves in place. Unlike a lot of internet start-ups who have to find an investor and 'blow it all on TV advertising', Simon already had a successful business under his belt and had already learnt the principles of being in business. He advises entrepreneurs to follow a 'no frills' policy to setting up.

When moneysupermarket.com was launched at the end of 1999, Simon felt he had created a truly useful site – the challenge now was to direct internet traffic to visit and use it. Despite having more money in the bank than most start-ups, there was no million pound fund to facilitate a vigorous TV advertising campaign so Simon and his team had to be more imaginative with their marketing strategy. He notes he was sure people would use the site, as he believes the average UK consumer is 'very price driven'. He explains, 'they like to shop around and to be able to tell their friend in the pub that they got a bargain'.

Growing interest

moneysupermarket.com makes its money every time a consumer clicks on a link to a financial provider such as Barclays or Capital One. So before moneysupermarket.com could make a profit from its site, it needed to set up deals with financial providers and convince them it could offer high quality internet leads. Simon remembers this process was extremely difficult – companies were of course very sceptical, as back then this method of partnership had never been attempted before.

moneysupermarket.com also anticipated that its information might be used by others, sourced through its website. The strategy was to pitch to the big web 'portals', such as BT, Yahoo and Freeserve (who already had lots of readers but relatively 'poor content', according to Simon), and offer them moneysupermarket.com's price comparison tools, splitting any e-commerce revenue 50:50. Simon approached the main players and pitched his novel idea, but was categorically turned down. The companies were not interested in a revenue share and were asking for a fee from him of millions up front, which moneysupermarket.com could not offer. Simon's last appointment in the first week of pitching was to the *Daily Mail*'s financial website, thisismoney.co.uk. They liked the content that moneysupermarket.com was offering so much that they took a gamble and agreed to a revenue share in early 2000.

Simon remembers how after this break, other portals 'sat up' and thought 'hang on a minute, they've got better information than us and they are our competitor'. Once they saw the information in practice, moneysupermarket.com secured the internet portals that had at first declined. Now, approximately 200 portals carry its content.

It also became much easier to set up deals with the financial providers that would provide the income, and Simon describes how the deals slowly 'dripped' in: 'once you have enough inertia behind you, they fall like a pack of cards'. A slow yet rewarding process, within six months (which seems like an age in the internet world) moneysupermarket. com had secured deals with five or six providers and therefore could start producing revenue.

Although moneysupermarket.com did no advertising, Simon did recognise the importance of good press coverage, as this was essential in driving traffic to the site. He recalls spending nearly £100,000 on PR, using both PR company Lansons, of London, and PR staff employed in-house. Simon ensured his researchers talked to all the national financial press every month – from *The Sunday Times* to the *Daily Star* – financial journalists would obtain figures and statistics from moneysupermarket.com and quote their source in articles. He 'knew straight away that this was one of the most effective ways to drive traffic and raise your profile'. Simon describes this endeavour as a 'little bit cleverer than just spending money on advertising'.

Although he faced a challenging start, Simon believes this was inevitable as he was pitching a unique idea, essential, he feels, to success. If your idea is not unique, it must at least be a variation of what exists in that market at the time. He believes that if you follow what everyone else is doing, 'how do you stand out?' moneysupermarket. com was the first price comparison tool for consumers in early 2000, and by the end of the same year had been joined by others cashing in on its success. Simon believes that because the company was first in the market it had the advantage, but it was crucial they capitalised on this: 'you have to put your foot down on the accelerator or people will catch you up very quickly'.

Moving with the times

In its first year, moneysupermarket.com made a respectable £500,000 and received around 50,000–60,000 hits a month. This surpassed expectations, but Simon adds the real surprise lies in the recent success of the company, which received nearly 120 million visitors to the money and travel websites and turned over more than £136m in 2009. In a way, Simon comments that moneysupermarket.com was a 'victim of its own success' as the servers crashed several times to begin with, due to underestimating the server capacity needed to cope with the amount of hits. Simon had to quickly adapt the servers to allow for the demand generated and he describes the 'steep learning curve' the company went through to rectify the problem.

moneysupermarket.com had one very close call: in 2001, the year of the dotcom boom, London bankers followed lastminute.com's example and advised Simon to float the business, estimating he would get £100m for it. Obviously intrigued by this estimate (turning over half a million a year), Simon started the long process of floating the company. However, not long after lastminute.com was floated, its shares crashed and the dotcom boom rapidly turned into a bust. moneysupermarket. com had to pull its floatation four weeks from completion and Simon remembers this was a very painful process that made him a more cautious businessman. Eventually, of course, the company did end up floating but this wasn't until 2007.

In 2002, Simon and his team developed some clever technology, which Simon admits was groundbreaking then but is probably commonplace now. It worked like a 'spider robot': after the consumer keys in their details, the robot searches hundreds of sites and brings back the results on one page, making the site faster, more efficient and fully inclusive in its searches.

Alongside this, the business branched into the insurance market with insuresupermarket.com in February 2003. Successful to the core, Simon proudly quotes that moneysupermarket.com is the largest broker in motor insurance policies, arranging 'something ridiculous' like 850,000 quotes per month. Later the same year, the company launched travelsupermarket.com and burst into the highly competitive travel market. This move may have been a risky one as this was a step out of the financial market they had dominated, yet Simon made sure travelsupermarket.com had something new to offer consumers – the technology ensured the site searched every travel provider including, for example, charter flights and aggregators, while existing sites only searched deals from the traditional airlines or agencies. Again, Simon ensured moneysupermarket.com differentiated itself from any competitors as it explored new markets.

Where are they now?

More than a decade later and the business has grown fantastically. In July 2007 the company floated on the London Stock Exchange with a market capitalisation of £843m, making it the biggest internet IPO in Europe. Simon netted £101m from the deal but retained more than 50% of the company shares.

Turnover reached £136.9m in 2009, the same year Simon stepped down from the day-to-day running of the business. He remains with the company as executive deputy chairman while working on other projects. Simon has also recently launched two new websites in the travel sector, Simonseeks and Simonscapes.

Gü Chocolate Puds
The sweet taste of success

CHOCOLATE PUDS

Founder: James Averdieck

Age at start: 37

Background: Worked for St Ivel for nine years in sales and marketing

Start year: 2003

Business: Desserts and puddings

James Averdieck, founder of Gü Chocolate Puds, the high quality desserts and puddings company, has cooked up a series of products that have found their way remarkably rapidly into over 3,000 supermarkets in the UK, as well as many other food retailers. James spotted a gap in the market: there was a serious lack of high quality desserts that could be bought and consumed at home. Since launching in 2003, Gü Chocolate Puds has grown into a business which generated revenues of £27m in 2010.

Entrepreneurial ambition

James had always wanted to be an entrepreneur, and other members of his family – his brothers, father, grandfather – had run their own businesses. 'It's in the blood' he says. He had run other ventures while he was at university and feels that it was only a matter of time before he did so again. His family have been a constant source of advice and his father drummed into him the belief that the key to a successful business was 'having the right product'. James says that the view might be obvious, but it is a crucial part of a business that many people fail to get right.

James noticed that many of the fine desserts found in the patisseries of France and Belgium were often not available in the UK. There were also very few brands associated with high quality desserts, and he thought the British public could do with one. It was an industry that he knew well as he was a member of the board at St Ivel, the desserts company, and had previous experience at Safeway.

He thought that British tastes were more sophisticated than the range on offer in most supermarkets suggested, and that, when it came down to it, 'Brits love a decent pudding'. He also believed that many people who hosted dinner parties were accustomed to eating at good restaurants, but perhaps lacked the skills or time to make their own pudding. Therefore, he mused, the chance to buy a ready-made but still top quality dessert would be popular with many people.

James decided to create a 'premium brand' that captured the essence of good chocolate and was the sort of food that you could buy in, for instance, a good patisserie in Paris.

James saw himself as more of a 'sales and marketing guy' so he knew he needed someone who could provide the food and manufacturing side of the business. However, while he was still working for St Ivel, he had come to know a company called Rensow Patisserie at a trade show in Spain in 2000. It was well established in the airline food industry and was looking to open up new lines of business.

In Rensow, he saw a business that could manufacture good quality food in an efficient way. James knew the retail market and was confident he could do the selling, so the partners felt that they 'covered all the bases'.

James mused over his idea for some time until in January 2003 the joint venture was put together with an initial investment of about £100,000. The company, which was later to become known as Gü, began creating its products based partly on the foods that James had sampled on the Continent.

The first product it designed was a chocolate pudding presented in a glass ramekin. James felt that the quality of the food and its presentation meant that it was of restaurant calibre; it could also be customised by the consumer and, perhaps, even passed off as their own creation.

'Gü is a really good solution to the question "what am I going to serve my guests for pudding?"' James asserts. 'It has a home-made quality but also it has a convenience as well.'

Creating the brand

Although James believed he had both a great product and that there was a gap in the market, he knew that in order to establish the business he would also require a great brand. Despite a background in sales and marketing himself, he felt his business needed something special, so he hired a branding company, Big Fish, who had experience in conceiving and designing premium brands, to design the packaging logos for his business and, perhaps most importantly, come up with the name.

He was in a good position to approach such a company as he knew the market that he was selling to and so he could outline his typical buyer to them. He took his product with him so the company could actually experience it for themselves. Big Fish was suitably impressed with James' product and wanted to work with him.

This was a considerable risk on James' part as he had to outlay a significant amount of money, and he was also putting the future of his company into someone else's hands. However, Big Fish had an impressive client list and showed considerable passion for James' business.

The director of Big Fish, Perry Haydn Taylor, loved James' product and conceived of the Gü brand himself. He decided to sell the brand to James in a somewhat unorthodox manner. Perry told James that the Gü brand would be perfect, however he also fabricated that it already belonged to a European company.

'They showed it to me and I thought "what a brilliant name, but . . . they've beaten us to it!" – I was totally hooked,' James remembers.

Certain that the brand was right Taylor revealed the truth and James took the name as his own. However, he wanted to test the brand out. So he took some of the early product boxes and cheekily slipped them on to the shelf of his local supermarket. He then stood back and watched the shoppers take them off the shelf – further proof that he was onto a winner.

James says, 'a brand encapsulates the essence of what you are selling: when I was shown Gü for the first time I just knew "that's us".'

Today, James refers to the Gü brand as his 'number one advertisement' and clearly has no regrets about his decision to get an expert in to do the branding.

'I think you have to seduce your customers twice: once with the packaging and then again with the product itself. If you do that you will have loyal customers,' James says.

Cracking the supermarkets

In order to sell Gü in the massive quantities that he wanted, James knew he had to get his products into the supermarkets. His previous experience in the market was, of course, a major benefit to him, but selling a new product to supermarkets from an unknown new company is a very tough nut to crack.

He knew from his experience at St Ivel that even if they liked the product, the supermarkets would need satisfying about lots of issues such as food safety, factory hygiene and ability to fulfil demand. However, as his business partner was already an established food manufacturer many of the tough questions could be confidently answered. Nevertheless, he was no longer working for St Ivel and was now the head of a new company with no prior history.

'Supermarket buyers aren't there to do your business plan for you. They are incredibly busy people and are approached constantly with new ideas. To stand out from the rest of the pack you need to offer real innovation.

'I feel also that it is really important that you actually get to meet the buyers so that they can see the passion that has gone into the product,' James suggests. 'In my case it was a question of calling the right people and immediately establishing credentials to get that initial meeting.'

Gü launched with Waitrose and Sainsbury's in June 2003. Others followed and a year later Gü was supplying puddings across the length and breadth of the country. However, despite Gü's success, James is determined to avoid becoming complacent. The battle for shelf space is continuous and there are always other products that are waiting, if yours do not work.

There is also the constant pressure of supplying stores seven days a week. Gü employed a distribution company to take on some of the strain but it was James' responsibility to ensure that the orders were fulfilled.

'Logistics in the UK are the most sophisticated in the world, and the most demanding,' he says. 'It is a case of monitoring what's going on and trying to piggy-back on other companies' deliveries by buying a bit of space in their trucks.'

Where are they now?

James Averdieck sold Gü to Noble Foods in January 2010 in deal worth £30m. At the time of the sale it was recording an annual turnover of £27m. James has remained at the company as a minority shareholder and is currently international director.

The product range has grown considerably since launching in 2003 and Gü now produces a variety of puddings, soufflés and ice cream. It also has a sister brand, Frü, which produces an impressive range of fruit-inspired luxury desserts.

Dreams
Live your dreams

Founder: Mike Clare

Age at start: 30

Background: Area manager in furniture retail

Start year: 1985

Business: Bed retailer

Mike Clare opened his first furniture store in Uxbridge in the summer of 1985, scraping together the money to get started. He always had 'big plans' for the company that began life as The Sofa Bed Centre; but in the years that have passed and after some serious re-branding, such plans have surely been eclipsed by a much more successful reality. Dreams has won Furniture Retailer of the Year three times, turns over a quarter of a billion pounds a year and, as it continues to grow, Dreams is now firmly established as Britain's leading bed specialist with nearly 250 bed superstores nationwide.

Reviving a dormant idea

Mike had been dreaming of running his own furniture retail company for a long time before he decided to leave his job as area manager at a local furniture store to start his own business. It was, he says, not a new idea and he had in fact even entered into talks with people 'way back before that' in the late 1970s, before realising he did not have enough of a business credit rating, funds or, in fact, the trust of his landlord to forge ahead. As a result, the idea lay dormant for the next five years before Mike decided, shortly after his 30th birthday, to take the plunge and start up a company that specialised in selling sofa beds.

According to Mike, a key business consideration is to have a good speciality product to focus on and sofa beds seemed to fit the bill nicely at that time. They were a new product, freshly imported from America and 'all the rage' amid the general market in the 1980s days of 'hopeless and uncomfortable' bed settees. They had also, he says, not yet been widely picked up by other retailers, which he discovered by scouring furniture shop adverts in places such as the *Yellow Pages*. It seemed an opportune time to develop this niche. While admittedly 'risky', Mike confesses that it was his gut feeling which ultimately spurred him on, for he had a strong belief he was meeting a demand in the market and his business could be a real success.

From fledgling to fighting

Every business needs money to get started, and Mike initially struggled to come up with the funds he needed. Calculating that he would probably need somewhere between £20,000 and £25,000 to fit out a shop and gain suppliers, he approached the bank to see if they could lend him the money – to which he was told that they would match whatever he himself could raise. As Mike remembers it, this totalled about £8,000: £2,000 from the sale of his car, £2,000 worth of savings and a £4,000 loan charged to his credit card – ostensibly for refitting a kitchen! Consequently, the initial funds that he had to invest in his own business were £16,000; at least £5,000 less than he had initially hoped. Although this was disheartening, Mike was far from put off. Today, he says, if you are starting up a business you must be determined to make it work no matter what difficulties or obstacles lie in your path. While many people, he says, seem deterred by the idea of taking a risk, if your house is on the line and you are really planning to put everything you have in, then you will, in fact, do 'whatever's necessary to make it work' and not be confined by difficulties, financial or otherwise.

After securing a loan, the next stage was to find a cheap property to lease as The Sofa Bed Centre's showroom. In April 1985, he found an old motor-parts store in Hillingdon, which he bought. It was cheap, he remembers, because it was in a 'terrible state'. Although he had

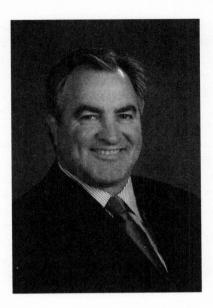

originally only intended to buy a small, single store, the landlord who leased the property also offered the property next door, saying the two together would only be 50% more than the initial rent. As a result, Mike ended up leasing both and knocking a big archway between the two – something he was glad of as he later found even the combined measurements were 1,000sq ft too small!

After initiating the buying of his property, Mike went to local libraries and looked in directories to find sofa-bed suppliers. He then rang them and asked if they would be happy to supply a new furniture business in a local area. Although there weren't many main suppliers of sofa beds, Mike ran into a common difficulty: the suppliers he spoke to were extremely reluctant to do business with a new company, due to the risk that they wouldn't get paid. However, using his initiative and persuasive personality, he eventually found one company which not only offered to supply him, but also offered much support, including a new set of supplier names for him to work from. Mike's experience suggests that slightly exaggerating the truth can sometimes pay off – by pretending to be a much larger company, he managed to gain lots of useful contacts and information. Ultimately his hard work and enthusiasm paid off, and a month before the opening of his store Mike had eight willing suppliers.

Now all he needed was customers. Mike believed strongly that his showroom was the key to attracting customers, and so he spent 18 hours a day there 'doing everything'. He enlisted the help of family members and Annette, who he found through an advertisement in his shop window before he opened, did the bookkeeping and finances.

Before opening he worked hard cleaning, re-carpeting, placing spotlights, receiving and displaying stock and pricing items. The pressure was on to open and to start taking money quickly, so Mike scheduled a 'Grand Opening' for mid-May, just a few weeks after taking possession of the store. Mike expected, naively with hindsight, that this would be the first day for everything, including trade. As a result, he was convinced that everything had to be perfect for that day.

Mike remembers fondly that the day before the opening one of the last things to arrive was a doormat – which he had ordered to replace the oil-stained one thathad been left. But when it arrived, it didn't fit in the concrete with the door opening over it, and so, refusing to be beaten, he spent the night on his hands and knees, chiselling the concrete down himself! Although amusing now, it is typical of the dedication every new business needs if it is to succeed; there simply was no alternative since the shop had to be ready for opening the next morning. When running a small business successfully you need to be willing and able to solve problems, whatever it takes.

It was finished in time, and the next morning Mike was shaking hands with the mayor in front of the local press and his newly opened The Sofa Bed Centre. He was lucky in that word had spread about the opening of the store. He had 'bigged it up' so much that images from the opening were even featured on the front page of one of the local papers the following day. And even more importantly, the shop made 10 sales that day!

That was when the next problem became clear – delivery and storage. Mike was using a local van man to deliver the orders but it was a few weeks before he realised that he couldn't fit all the stock he was having delivered into the showroom. To overcome this he managed to rent some space in the back of a nearby industrial unit to store the sofa beds until they were due to be delivered to customers. This is typical of Mike's approach to business – addressing each problem as it crops up and focusing on it determinedly until it is solved.

The sales carried on, with the first month's reaching an impressive £30,000; the first year's sales were £400,000. In 1985, this was far more than a normal shop. Mike generated enough profit to finance the opening of a second store that November. After the experience from his first store, Mike made sure the next was much bigger and had its own storage area out the back to make delivery much easier.

Landlords need to know that their rent is going to be paid, and usually look at a prospective tenant's 'covenant', which means its reputation and ability to pay. Once a business has lots of shops it is easy for landlords to check that other landlords are being paid on time, but for new businesses this is obviously not possible. The fact that The Sofa Bed Centre was now trading made it far easier to persuade a landlord to accept Mike as a tenant for the second shop. Having a second property meant expansion thereafter was much easier; as a result, sales continued strongly. By the end of the second year, The Sofa Bed Centre had expanded into five stores.

During one of Mike's monthly meetings with key staff, the limitations of The Sofa Bed Centre were discussed. To Mike, sofa beds seemed too much of a niche product and he wanted to expand into selling something else. According to him, the 'obvious' product to sell alongside sofa beds was either sofas or beds – and beds seemed the natural answer; they were an easier shape to fit in vans and as we all spend a third of our life in one, the product appeals to everybody. Mike also decided to change the name of the company to Dreams Ltd, a name which Mike likens to Virgin in that it doesn't mean any one thing and can be used to brand more than one product. He promptly registered the company and got ready to trade under the new name.

Expansion nightmares

It was literally on the first day of trading as Dreams Ltd, in 1987, when the company encountered its next problem: an injunction, delivered by motorbike. Mike was told by the messenger that this injunction meant the company would have to stop trading under the name, Dreams Ltd, as there was another company called Dreams which was selling beds already. Mike managed to persuade the other business that both companies could trade as Dreams until a court case to decide who was allowed to use the name long term. Mike's Dreams fought this court case over a long time, trading successfully all the while, and eventually winning the rights by default after the other company went bust. From this point Dreams went from strength to strength.

Living the dream

Since the beginning, Dreams' success had been swift, and surprising. Mike found that although selling beds did not bring in big money instantly, it is such a big market that it proved 'easier' than he had thought, with sales in the first week of trading with the new name and range hitting £15,000 and quickly rising thereafter. Mike attributes this steady progression in part to learning from his mistakes. So while it bought some beds that didn't sell or weren't sufficiently well-made early on, Dreams continually adapted, changed and concentrated on putting things right. This willingness to change is key to many entrepreneurs' success. Eventually, even though Dreams had begun by selling both sofa beds and beds, the beds began to do so well and took up so much space in the showroom that the sofa beds took something of a backseat, leaving Dreams focused on becoming Britain's leading bed specialist.

It is a reputation that Mike has been careful to cultivate and maintain over the years, and all the evidence points to its success. Between 2002 and 2003 alone, Dreams increased its store tally by a third, totalling 100 stores, and then expanded by beginning to manufacture some of its own beds, supplying to businesses such as nursing homes and hotels. Dreams is responsible for opening the largest bed store in the world, in the West Midlands, and now operates 240 stores in total.

Where are they now?

Mike Clare stepped down as chief executive of Dreams after selling the company to Exponent Private Equity in 2008, in a deal worth a reported £230m. He remains a shareholder and non-executive president. In 2010, the company recorded an operating profit of £18.4m on sales of £280m in its 240 UK stores.

Since its humble beginnings as The Sofa Bed Centre, Dreams is now recognised as the UK's biggest bed retailer. The company has a successful website and has expanded its product range further into other bedroom furniture.

Dyson
Designing from dust

dyson

Founder:	James Dyson
Age at start:	45
Background:	Designer and inventor
Start year:	1992
Business:	Vacuum cleaner manufacturer

Today, Dyson is very much a household name; it advertises its revolutionary products prominently on television, they are on sale throughout the world, and its every move is written up in the national press. Yet two decades ago, you literally couldn't buy a Dyson vacuum cleaner anywhere in Britain. James Dyson prefers to think of himself as a designer rather than an entrepreneur; in fact, he excels at both. The business he founded currently exports to over 40 countries, and has achieved sales of more than £3bn worldwide. Yet it all started with one man and an idea.

To accomplish this, James endured 20 years of debt, faced multiple lawsuits and learnt countless lessons on the temperamental nature of vacuum cleaner licensing agreements.

Innovative pedigree

James Dyson is an engineer and designer. While studying at the Royal College of Art, James developed his dream: to be a modern day Brunel and to revolutionise the way products are designed. James' first product, his graduation piece, was the Sea Truck, which he designed for British inventor and entrepreneur Jeremy Fry in 1969. The Sea Truck was sold in more than 50 countries and has achieved sales of over $500m to date. Jeremy gave James his first job, at Rotork Engineering, after he graduated and James was promoted to director just three years later. In this position, James discovered the difficulty of selling the commercially unfinished Sea Truck and learnt the importance of perfecting a design before commencing its production.

In 1974 James chose to pursue inventing for himself, and left Rotork to design the award-winning Ballbarrow, a deviation from the wheelbarrow, using a pneumatic balloon in place of the usual wheel. James believed he could modernise the traditional barrow, and so he left a highly paid, prestigious job. Throughout his career James has been driven by a desire to make technology work better.

He needed capital to fund his first venture, and persuaded two wealthy people he knew (one who was his brother-in-law) to invest, and Kirk-Dyson was founded. By March 1974 they had a prototype, but six months into production the manufacturer they had chosen began raising its prices, leading to a decision to borrow another £45,000 to buy machinery from America and manufacture it themselves.

Here, James had his first taste of selling consumer goods. A journalist from *The Sunday Times* picked up on the invention: James notes the power that a 'tried and tested' article can have on sales, proving a product's worth. Soon, they were selling 45,000 Ballbarrows and turning over £600,000 a year. The company tried to export its products to America to grow sales, but ended up in a costly lawsuit with an American business which had produced a very similar product after taking on one of James' staff.

Cleaning conundrum

During this time, James was renovating his house in the Cotswolds and was amazed at the inefficiency of his vacuum cleaner. Surprisingly, there seemed to be no obvious improvement if he used a new bag. Even investing in the most advanced model on the market, it clogged after use in just a few rooms, losing its suction. At Ballbarrow's factory, he was experiencing similar problems on a much larger scale: the industrial cleaner was also clogging up with dust during production.

James found out that cyclones were often used for large-scale industrial cleaning, and was quoted £75,000 to install one.

Instead of paying this colossal sum, James was inspired by a 30ft cyclone at a nearby sawmill that spun dust out of the air by a centrifugal force. After putting this technology to the test at the factory, James realised the potential of a miniature version of this to solve his domestic problem. He ripped the bag off his vacuum cleaner and 'rigged up a rudimentary cardboard cyclone' with cereal packets and masking tape. This foetal prototype essentially worked and drove James to seriously consider the potential of this creation.

Taking this idea first to the Kirk-Dyson board, presenting an opportunity to diversify from the limited gardening market into domestic appliances, James was met with pessimism. Not long after, financial friction eventually led to James being ousted from Kirk-Dyson by the other shareholders. As Ballbarrow's patent was owned by the company, not the designer, James left without his design – a mistake he vowed never to repeat.

Alone again, James had to rely on his unswerving belief in his theoretical product; there was nothing to prove a cyclonic vacuum cleaner would work yet, and no evidence to persuade investors. Still, he set about designing one, through the gruelling process of trial and error. Shunned by his business partners and in need of financial backing, James approached an old friend with his prospective invention. Jeremy Fry provided £25,000, which James doubled by borrowing against his home. So James set up the Air Power Vacuum Cleaner Company, and began experimenting in an old, draughty coach house next to his home.

For five long years he toiled over the design, attempting to develop his idea and win investment to construct his product. In 1983, after making more than 5,000 prototypes, he came up with a design which worked perfectly. Unlike most vacuum cleaners, which used a bag to store any dirt they collected, James' design used two cyclones to separate the dust from the air to stop the machine from clogging.

James explains that he was sure he had a mass-market design. Originally, James had intended the Air Power Vacuum Cleaner Company to manufacture the products itself, yet due to the lengthy and costly process, the company was deeply in debt and James was exhausted. Changing the company name to Prototypes Ltd, the business partners changed tack, now opting just to invent, and not manufacture. In the same year, the vacuum graced the cover of *Design* magazine, festooned in bright pink plastic.

Sucking up the courage

Having made its debut, James needed to find a manufacturer, ideally in Britain or Europe. James visited all the established manufacturers but surmised that although many companies understood his design, their main concern was to protect their own models: he was met with 'a staggering reluctance' to invest in new technology. Offering tools that would change the realm of cleaning forever, James recalls with understandable frustration that 'they seemed more interested in maintaining the status quo – and of course, selling bags': the vacuum bag market was valued at £100m a year in the UK alone in 1984.

Although a few manufacturers did eventually offer to license his design, knowing the significance of his technology, James was unwilling to accept the 'paltry percentages' they offered, despite being in dire financial need of the customary payment he would have got when a deal was signed. It would have been easy to sell his technology in a one-off payment but after the Ballbarrow experience, he was adamant that this time he would retain ownership. James also suspected that if he succumbed, his design would get swept under the carpet and never be made. Jeremy Fry's Rotork came to his aid for a brief spell in 1983 and manufactured a few hundred vacuum cleaners. Although this was a long way off the mass production James envisaged, significantly, the first ever models were manufactured and sold.

Meanwhile, James was still working hard trying to secure deals, always being disappointed when they fell through, mostly due to licensing disagreements. Aware that business culture in America was much more conducive to new technology, he started targeting the American market. Yet again, deals fell through with Black & Decker and Conair, both at the last minute. A deal was signed with Amway in April 1984, a cause for celebration, but within a matter of months it withdrew from the contract, accusing Prototypes Ltd of deceiving it as the product was not yet ready. A legal battle ensued lasting eight months, denying James the opportunity to re-license his product elsewhere until early 1985. He settled quickly due to legal costs and had to give back everything Amway had paid him, but eventually was free.

After these demoralising years, James was desperate to manufacture the cleaner himself, but financing this while the company was so heavily in debt was impossible: his only hope was to succeed in licensing his technology to one country to generate an income which he could use to fund his own manufacturing.

Eventually, in 1985, James stumbled upon a Japanese manufacturer offering him a reasonable deal. He sold the rights to the technology in Japan and at last began manufacturing vacuum cleaners. The machine, named 'G-Force', went on to win the 1991 International Design Fair prize in Japan and so impressed were Japanese consumers with the model that it became a status symbol and sold for $2,000 a pop.

With a retail product on the shelves, albeit not in the UK, James hired a small team of graduates from the Royal College of Art to develop the product in his coach house-turned-workshop; James imagined it would be easier to sell a ready-made product in America. However in 1987, as he was just about to sign a deal with Canadian company Iona to manufacture a carpet-cleaning version of the design, he discovered that Amway, the manufacturing juggernaut that had pulled out of a deal three years earlier, had begun producing vacuums with the cyclone design. James began what turned into a five-year legal battle, which meant that he had to spend all his royalties from the Japanese company on legal fees. More successfully, he also secured an agreement to sell his technology in the commercial market, and Johnson Wax launched an industrial cleaner.

In the early 1990s, the royalties from Japanese and finally American sales placated the company's bank manager and made the prospect of manufacturing in Britain vaguely feasible once more. The lawsuit with Amway had been settled, relieving funds but not enough to go into business alone.

James approached potential investors, but was categorically turned down because of the 'whimsical' idea of a designer running a business. What would *Dragons' Den* have made of him, I wonder? Multiple applications for a bank loan were also dismissed, until eventually a sympathetic bank manager wangled James a £600,000 loan, guaranteed by a mortgage on his homes in London and Bath.

Product perfection

In 1992, James recruited design engineers from the RCA to work on what he called the Dual Cyclone™ design, which was to be, for the first time, manufactured in his own name. Determined to perfect the design before its release, the team took their time, even though competitors were copying some of their unpatented design elements. In the long run, James believes, this paid off, and the perfectionist designer released an unrushed, finished version.

The first DC01 was completed on 2 May 1992, James' 45th birthday. Its fundamental design, not only the technology, differentiated from other vacuum cleaners: early market research had suggested the consumer did not want a clear bin, yet now, it is one of the make's most popular features and competitors are copying it. James sold it from a practical perspective – you could see the machine working, and knew when it needed to be emptied.

To be able to manufacture, still more money was needed, so James decided to sell all the rights to his technology to the manufacturer in Japan. This generated nearly all of the £900,000 he needed to go into production: Dyson Ltd was born.

As production began, Dyson Ltd's first sale was made in July 1992 to Great Universal Stores, the largest mail-order group in Britain. James recalls that after six hours of negotiations, he finally admitted to its chief buyer that he found its catalogue boring and felt it needed an injection of new technology, in the form of his Dyson DC01 cleaner. He reminisces that this candid approach 'finally sealed the deal – he took a thousand'. From this success, the company secured contracts with catalogue companies such as Littlewoods; initially he was cautious not to approach the high-street retailers in case competitors got wind of the impending launch. James scrapped this strategy when John Lewis asked to take 250 DC01s.

As James and his team concentrated on selling, small, independent Italian tooling companies were contracted to make the gargantuan moulds needed in production and by the end of November 1992, the tools were transported to Wales, where Phillips Plastics was to produce the machines. Efficient workmanship meant the first DC01s came off the production line in January 1993. In April, a big order from Rumbelows set Dyson up with a solid base of orders: the future looked rosy.

However, on the rocky path to success, the manufacturer, Phillips, vastly raised its prices, forcing Dyson to gradually move production elsewhere. As happened so often in this story, a lawsuit ensued and forced Dyson to stop manufacturing for one crucial month. Yet again refusing to be defeated, James and his team quickly set up a production factory in an old Royal Mail warehouse and produced the very first DC01 exclusively made by a Dyson Ltd employee, in July 1993.

Fifteen years after his sawmill epiphany, James finally had his own business manufacturing his revolutionary cleaner. He had spent the staggering sums of £1.5m on patents and £2m–£3m on development.

James believes that in the UK there is a tendency to over-value marketing, when 'having well-engineered products does the work for you – it speaks for itself'. With an unassailable design, and manufacturing in place, surely Dyson could sit back and watch consumers consume. Yet they were wary of buying an unknown brand, and shops promoted traditional models. Still, word spread as the 'intrinsic excellence of the machine' spoke for itself, receiving much acclaim through editorial coverage without a rigid advertising campaign. In under a year, Dyson Ltd turned over £2.4m and after one year of retail, this had risen considerably to £9m.

Through the first few years of retail, sales grew healthily, but only really took off when superstores Comet and Currys started to sell the DC01, which they did in 1995. Almost immediately, the DC01 became the best-selling vacuum cleaner in the UK, where it has stayed ever since.

On the verge of bankruptcy many times and frequently in the face of great adversity, James' unswerving belief in his groundbreaking technology prevailed. He explains that 'engineering and design are the driving forces behind everything I do'.

Where are they now?

James Dyson is still the sole owner of Dyson Ltd, which recorded an operating profit of £190m from sales of £770m in 2010. The company employs more than 2,500 staff worldwide and is currently working to double the number of its engineers in a bid to retain its reputation for delivering pioneering new products.

Dyson Ltd continues to innovate and offer consumers new alternatives to old appliances, such as the recently launched bladeless Air Multiplier fan. Boasting 40% of British vacuum cleaner sales, the company has made its founder a billionaire. The brand is now also a market leader in several international markets including North America, France, Spain and New Zealand.

JoJo Maman Bébé
Convalescent
inspiration

JoJo Maman Bébé
maternity | baby and child | nursery and toys

Company: JoJo Maman Bébé

Founder: Laura Tenison

Age at start: 25

Background: Clothes making and property development

Start year: 1992

Business: Maternity and baby clothes retailer

t's not often that car accidents can take credit for inspiring new businesses, but a particularly bad smash which left Laura Tenison seriously injured with 20 broken bones, did just that. Now the business she built afterwards, a mail-order and retail business supplying pregnancy wear and children's clothing, has won awards, built a high street presence all round the UK, and made a fortune for the ambitious and determined Laura.

Finding and funding her passion

According to Laura, her entrepreneurial skills were sharpened from a young age, even making dolls clothes in exchange for pocket money at the age of eight. She remembers always being keen to run her own business, and acquired her own sewing machine by the time she was 13 to take orders for made-to-measure wedding dresses. Later, she did an 18-month apprenticeship at Aquascutum, then went on to make and sell haute couture men's clothing. She was clearly a natural fit for the rag trade, and so, aged 22, she was determined to launch her own clothing business.

However, while the skills and the self-belief were there, Tension had no capital to set up a new clothing business. As a result, she decided to get into the property market in France with the view, ultimately, to building up a good business which she could sell to fund the clothing manufacturing company she dreamed of. Despite having no experience in property, Laura had noticed a gap in the market on a trip to France: selling, renovating and letting houses in France to British clients. She felt that she would be able to channel her French language skills and the experience she'd gained doing up her own flat in London into filling that gap. The lucrative property market was, she says, 'a good way in' to starting a clothing line as it had low start-up costs and overheads. She could thus afford to start the property company with just £2,000, borrowed from one of her brothers, which was handy as the high street banks turned down her request for a loan.

After travelling around rural France to find suitable properties to let, Laura would find British clients by putting advertisements in the UK press. She ran this business for three years and sold it in 1992. The sale of this business raised about £70,000 for Laura, who then persuaded a bank to match it with a £70,000 loan with the view, at last, to setting up a clothing manufacturing company. Although Laura knew she wanted to set up some sort of clothing company she says that she was still at this time unsure as to what area she would be focusing on, and was indeed quite open to ideas.

The birth of JoJo

The idea that became JoJo Maman Bébé came to her in a remarkable way. At Easter-time in 1992, Laura was involved in such a bad car accident in France that she was flown by air ambulance back to the UK with two broken legs, crushed ribs, a shattered foot and damage to her cheeks and jaw, confined to hospital for a long rehabilitation process thereafter. Because the orthopaedic ward she was due to stay in had no beds, Laura recounts how she was transferred to a cancer ward shortly after her arrival. It was here that she met the woman she credits with providing the inspiration for JoJo Maman Bébé, 'the one-stop-shop for all your maternity, baby and nursery needs'.

According to Laura, sometime during her recovery – when she was 'compos mentis again' – she got talking to the woman in the bed beside her and discovered that she was a 32-year-old mother with two young girls who she wished to purchase some clothes for. She was upset, Laura recalls, because while she was too ill to leave hospital, she could not find anything she considered nice in any of the mail-order catalogues, complaining to Laura that what was available was often limited and of a poor quality.

Although Laura had no experience in the childrenswear market and was not a mother herself, she recognised that this lady's comments might be just the fantastic business opportunity she was looking for. As a result, she describes how she plotted an early release from hospital, and once out – despite still being in a wheelchair – started work immediately.

The first thing she did was look into whether the complaints raised by her hospital neighbour were experienced by other young mothers. Was this really a gap in the market? She concluded, of course, that it was, and she set out to fill it.

Laura printed 10,000 questionnaires and used a mailing list of people interested in childrenswear for her research – which she says now was far too many (300 might be a more sensible number!). This research taught Laura several key points about her chosen market. First, she noted that while people did certainly want nice children's clothes, what they predominantly wanted was maternity wear because, she says, 'there was nothing nice and fashionable at that time'. She also found that as well as there being a definite gap in the market, the timing looked to be spot on: in 1992 Britain was experiencing something of a 'baby boom', while the economy was in deep recession. Laura found that many career mums who were being made redundant were finding this an opportune time to have a family and not return to work, thus the birth rate was 'flying'.

After conducting this research, Laura acted fast and drew up some designs for clothing she thought would be appropriate. She then set to work seeking to find another company to do the manufacturing and hired two part-time employees who could assist her with taking orders, modelling the samples, overseeing their warehouse and eventually, dispatching orders.

According to Tension, she decided to sell the clothing via mail-order as she wanted the company to become 'as mass-market as possible' and maternity wear was already something of a niche market, with approximately 500,000 women a year falling pregnant.

The name for the company came from her desire to find a brand name that was appropriate for both adult and children's clothing. 'JoJo' was chosen as a unisex baby name and 'Maman Bébé', French for mother and baby, derives from her time spent in France and her love of the country. From this amalgamation, the rather poetic JoJo Maman Bébé was born.

Teething problems

After putting her collection together, Laura then turned her attention to finding suppliers. This, she says, was where she encountered her first real problem. Although she had had some experience licensing haute couture clothing which, as made-to-measure pieces, could be produced on a smaller scale, she found that the mass-market was a different story. Factories in China required minimum orders of 2,000 units per style, while factories in Europe needed 3,500. Laura knew that starting a new business was risky, and wanted to limit the risks, so wanted to make just 50 units per style initially, hoping, ultimately, to grow JoJo Maman Bébé to mass-market levels. Because of her ambitions, she wished to avoid using small manufacturers, who she says tended to charge too much anyway, which would hurt her ability to make a profit.

It was while doing the rounds at a trade fair in Paris that Laura, who has always been committed to ethical trading, found the answer to this problem by way of a delegation from Columbia. To promote non-drugs trade, the EEC had recently suspended import tax on Columbian produce for a short period meaning that the cost of importation to

Britain would be cheaper. When Laura approached the representatives to enquire how much they would charge to produce 50 of a given design, she found the prices they offered her were reasonable.

Some of the designs were more complex than others, however, needing more labour to make. Initially, Laura decided to produce these pieces (which she did not want to commission large quantities of) using the Columbian supplier, while also making 'bits and pieces' in France. Although it was not a long-term solution, since Laura confesses that she ultimately wanted to manufacture in Europe, this was an excellent way to get started, enabling her to produce small quantities of early designs cost-effectively.

The other step that Laura obviously had to take when launching her mail-order business was to create a catalogue. This was of the utmost importance, she points out, as anyone launching a mail-order company is required to put 'absolutely everything into catalogue production' in the hope of securing sales from it; not only is it a huge financial investment for any mail-order business, it also determines whether or not the business will succeed. Consequently, after the collection was designed and made, models – ex-professionals who were friends of friends – were cast and the layout was decided. The actual graphic design element was outsourced to a friend who ran a graphic design company conveniently located in the office which they shared. Later, this friend's company did not work out as intended and the friend ultimately came to work at JoJo Maman Bébé full-time.

Next, Laura set to work compiling a mailing list, starting with the names that she had gathered while conducting her market research. She then wrote a press release – despite having had no previous experience – by copying the format from a friend who worked in a press office. According to Laura, this is the way one must always play it: you should never let the fact that you're inexperienced get in your way. In her own words: 'if you don't know how to do it, ask people and work it out for yourself'.

First steps

The timing was just right and JoJo Maman Bébé made its way quickly into the press. Laura attributes this to there being very few 'fashionable' maternity wear collections around at that time and that what JoJo Maman Bébé was doing was exciting and new. Laura recalls, in particular, such innovative, early ideas included making a maternity version of the black business suit. In those days, she says, companies designing maternity wear tended to produce frumpy clothing such as tent dresses and dungarees and would always avoid black due to 'mad superstitions' that wearing black might somehow cause you to miscarry. But when Laura commissioned such items, she found that various niche groups picked it up and that people responded well; as a result she says that part of creating a successful business is sticking your neck out and not being afraid to try something new.

It is a plan that has brought the company much success. In JoJo Maman Bébé's first year it sent out 30,000 catalogues and sold clothes worth £50,000, a figure which increased five-fold in the following year to £250,000. It has not, however, always been plain sailing; 18 months into JoJo Maman Bébé's lifespan, the pound devalued by 10% causing all of Laura's purchases, made primarily abroad, to become more expensive. Because the profit margin at that time was less than that, Laura was left in a situation where she had to raise more capital. The banks, she remembers, would not look at her, having already matched the £70,000 she had put up at the start of the previous year. As a result, Laura re-mortgaged her house, as she was convinced of the success of the company; she believed it had the sales but was just under-financed. While Laura ultimately made the money back, she admits that mortgaging her house was, of course, not part of the original plan and as a result she warns those who are starting their own business to always have a contingency allowance to cover the costs if a disaster should ever strike.

Despite such problems, faith in the company has certainly paid off. After its second year, JoJo Maman Bébé began growing at an average yearly pace of 25%, far exceeding Laura's initial expectations of 10–15% a year. She suggests part of the reason for the success was the fact that she put her business plan into action quickly, at a time when the market was relatively untapped and there was a definite demand for her product. She does, however, point out that since that time, the market has become 'saturated' with competitors and there is now a large variety of both good and bad maternity wear. This, she says, has meant that JoJo Maman Bébé has had to be 'very good' in order to survive.

Laura recommends, first, taking educated risks when you know you can afford them, a key example being the decision to move into retail in 2004. While this was itself a risk, Laura describes how, by building up a database of nearly a million customers, she was able to ascertain where the main buyers were located and concentrate store locations in nearby 'local' shopping areas that customers could access easily. Laura also suggests a focus on the negative rather than positive aspects of the business as a means of ensuring high standards. By having the grit to focus in on problem areas in your business, and not backing away until they're solved, she says you will ultimately help to ensure the future of your company.

Where are they now?

Laura Tenison is still heavily involved with JoJo Maman Bébé, which has successfully launched high street shops and a website from which customers can buy its goods. It currently has more than 35 stores nationwide, with more opening regularly. Laura was made an MBE in the Queen's New Year's Honours List in 2004 for services to business, while more recent accolades include being named Female Entrepreneur of the Year at the Fast Growth Business Awards in 2007 and being awarded the prestigious Veuve Clicquot Business Woman of the Year title in 2010. Similarly, the company has received countless awards within the industry, including the Fast Growth Business Awards' Retail Business of the Year in 2007.

In May 2011, Laura announced the sale of a minority stake in the business to private equity firm Magenta Partners for an undisclosed amount. Before the deal, the company enjoyed a 50% increase in revenue taking it from £18m to £27m in the two years between 2009 and 2011. And on a personal and business level, Laura and JoJo Maman Bébé co-fund Nema, a children's charity in Mozambique, for which she is a trustee.

How They Started

How 30 good ideas became great businesses

As well as the nine in this book the original *How They Started* also contains the start-up stories of the following companies:

Cobra Beer

The Black Farmer

The Fabulous Bakin' Boys

S&A Foods

Cotton Traders

One Small Step One Giant Leap

Hotel Du Vin

The Cinnamon Club

Bebo

Friends Reunited

Vitabiotics

Codemasters

Dorling Kindersley

Extreme Group

MeetingZone

Sage

Psion Teklogix

Hargreaves Lansdown

Jigsaw Research

Pimlico Plumbers

The SG Group

How
They
Started

How 30 good ideas
became great businesses

innocent · GÜ · COBRA · Cotton TRADERS · Dreams

dyson · PSION · sage · DK · PIZZA EXPRESS

David Lester
Foreword by Richard Reed, innocent Drinks

&& Inspired
me to think
more about
my dreams
to start
a business
myself **""**

Amazon reader
review

How They Started
Global Brands

How 21 good ideas became great global businesses

In *How They Started: Global Brands*, you can enjoy the start-up stories of some of the world's most successful and internationally renowned companies:

adidas	Hilton Hotels
Billabong	Ikea
Cloudy Bay	Apple
The Coca-Cola Company	BlackBerry (RIM)
Green & Blacks	Nintendo
KFC	Nokia
Pizza Hut	Sony
Dyson	Bebo
Volvo Cars	eBay
Dorling Kindersley	Google
Lonely Planet	

" I certainly wish we'd had this book when we were starting innocent **"**

Richard Reed,
Joint founder,
innocent Drinks

How They Started in Tough Times

How 25 companies started and thrived during an economic crisis

In *How They Started in Tough Times*, the third book in the series, find out exactly how some of the world's most successful companies launched and thrived during times of economic crisis. In this book you can read about:

The Walt Disney Company

Penguin

Impressions

Three Sixty Entertainment

Mumsnet

Wikipedia

LinkedIn

IBM

Hewlett Packard

Microsoft

MeetingZone

Whole Foods Market

Specsavers

Moonpig

Jane Asher Cakes

Charlton House Catering

Masala Masala

KitcattNohr Alexander Shaw

We Are Social

Marmalade PR

Impact International

Foxtons

dunnhumby

Red or Dead

Go Sustainable

“ I wish
I had read
this book
ten years
ago... it shows
you why you
shouldn't put
off starting
your business
just because
we are in a
recession **”**

Nick Jenkins,
founder, Moonpig

About **Startups.co.uk**

Startups.co.uk is the UK's largest and most popular online resource for people starting their own business. It has more than 10,000 pages of independently written, practical advice and information designed to guide you through every step of starting up.

From formulating an idea, to writing a business plan, raising finance, finding suppliers and reaching customers, you'll find everything you need to make your first key decisions as a business owner.

In addition, we have more than 50 'How to start...' guides detailing every aspect of starting up an array of different businesses – from qualifications you'll need to the cost of equipment and rent. Whether you're looking to become an eBay entrepreneur or want to know what's involved in starting and running a nursery, our guides have got it covered.

The UK's top entrepreneurs frequently talk to **Startups.co.uk** and you'll be able to read, listen and watch videos of the likes of Peter Jones, Luke Johnson, Alan Sugar, Stelios Haji Ioannou and Richard Branson telling their inspirational stories.

With an interactive forum, **Startups.co.uk** also offers you the unique chance to network with other new business owners and raise your profile on a platform that attracts more than 150,000 visitors each month.

www.startups.co.uk

startups

build a better business

**Every year
we help
1.8 million
start-up
and small
business
owners**

ONLINE >

"You'd be mad not
to look at this site
if you want to
start a business"

The Times

10,000
pages of
trusted, expert
business
advice

FORUM >

Join our lively
community to
support all your
start-up efforts

startups.co.uk/forum

Over
37,000
members

AWARDS >

Celebrating
the UK's best
start-up businesses

startupsawards.co.uk

16
categories
championing
true talent

www.startups.co.uk *There's no better place to start than Startups*